78632

Come Sing God's Song

Thomas Paul Thigpen Illustrated by Joyce John

Chariot Books
DAVID C COOK PUBLISHING CO

Chariot Books is an imprint of David C. Cook Publishing Co.
David C. Cook Publishing Co., Elgin, Illinois 60120
David C. Cook Publishing Co., Weston, Ontario

COME SING GOD'S SONG
© 1987 by Thomas Paul Thigpen for the text and Joyce John for
the illustrations.
Designed by Jill Novak
First printing, 1987
Printed in Singapore
91 90 89 88 87   5 4 3 2 1

r Lydia, a worshiper of God

rary of Congress Cataloging-in-Publication Data
ggpen, Thomas Paul, 1954-
Come sing God's song.
Summary: Presents a song in praise of God and His world.
1. Praise of God—Juvenile literature. 2. Nature—Religious
pects—Christianity—Juvenile literature. [1. Hymns] I. John,
ce, ill. II. Title.
4817.T46 1987   242'.62   86-24197
3N 1-55513-052-6

Come sing God's song at the daybreak;
sing for the dawn of the day:
an orange and red song,
a get-out-of-bed song,
a song to start out on our way.

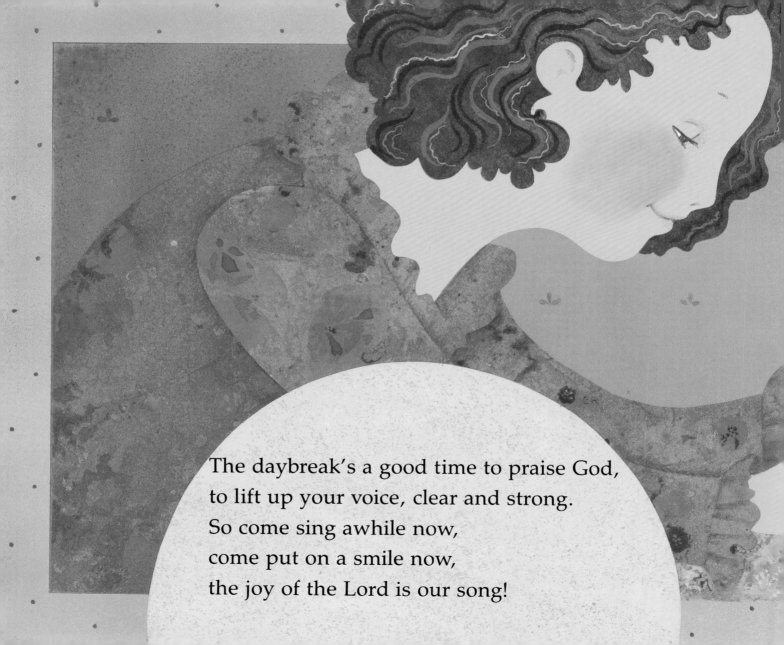

The daybreak's a good time to praise God,
to lift up your voice, clear and strong.
So come sing awhile now,
come put on a smile now,
the joy of the Lord is our song!

Come sing God's song through the morning,
sing for the chores to be done:
a sparkling white song,
a clean, shiny-bright song,
a song to turn work into fun.

The morning's a good time to praise God,
to lift up your voice, clear and strong.
So come sing awhile now,
come put on a smile now,
the joy of the Lord is our song!

Come sing God's song at the midday;
sing for the food that we eat:
a yellow and green song,
a corn-lima-bean song,
a song for the fruit, fresh and sweet.

The midday's a good time to praise God,
to lift up your voice, clear and strong.
So come sing awhile now,
come put on a smile now,
the joy of the Lord is our song!

Come sing God's song in the late day;
come singing all afternoon:
a black and a brown song,
a dusty playground song,
a busy and beautiful tune.

The late day's a good time to praise God,
to lift up your voice, clear and strong.
So come sing awhile now,
come put on a smile now,
the joy of the Lord is our song!

Come sing God's song in the evening;
sing for the face at your door:
a purple and gray song,
a ''how-was-your-day'' song;
we're home all together once more.

The evening's a good time to praise God,
to lift up your voice, clear and strong.
So come sing awhile now,
come put on a smile now,
the joy of the Lord is our song!

Come sing God's song in the nighttime;
sing for the stars and the moon:
a silver and blue song,
"good-night-I-love-you" song;
the morning will come again soon.

The nighttime's a good time to praise God,
to lift up your voice, clear and strong.
So come sing awhile now,
come put on a smile now,
the joy of the Lord is our song!

It's always a good time to praise God,
to lift up your voice, clear and strong.
So come sing awhile now,
come put on a smile now,
the joy of the Lord is our song!

Come Sing God's Song

Text by Thomas Paul Thigpen

Music by Tony L. Payne

2 Come sing God's song through the morning,
 sing for the chores to be done:
 a sparkling white song,
 a clean, shiny-bright song,
 a song to turn work into fun.
 The morning's a good time to praise God,
 to lift up your voice, clear and strong.
 So come sing awhile now,
 come put on a smile now,
 the joy of the Lord is our song!

3 Come sing God's song at the midday;
 sing for the food that we eat:
 a yellow and green song,
 a corn-lima-bean song,
 a song for the fruit, fresh and sweet.
 The midday's a good time to praise God,
 to lift up your voice, clear and strong.
 So come sing awhile now,
 come put on a smile now,
 the joy of the Lord is our song!

4 Come sing God's song in the late day;
 come singing all afternoon:
 a black and a brown song,
 a dusty playground song,
 a busy and beautiful tune.

The late day's a good time to praise God,
to lift up your voice, clear and strong.
So come sing awhile now,
come put on a smile now,
the joy of the Lord is our song!

5 Come sing God's song in the evening;
 sing for the face at your door:
 a purple and gray song,
 a "how-was-your-day" song;
 we're home all together once more.
 The evening's a good time to praise God,
 to lift up your voice, clear and strong.
 So come sing awhile now,
 come put on a smile now,
 the joy of the Lord is our song!

6 Come sing God's song in the nighttime;
 sing for the stars and the moon:
 a silver and blue song,
 "good-night-I-love-you" song;
 the morning will come again soon.
 The nighttime's a good time to praise God,
 to lift up your voice, clear and strong.
 So come sing awhile now,
 come put on a smile now,
 the joy of the Lord is our song!

The artist prepared this book using a collage process,
cutting the illustrations from papers she colored and textured.